Don't Blame God

Kenneth E. Hagin

Chapter 1
"WHY ME?"

Often, before you can receive anything from God, you must find answers to the questions that are keeping you from receiving. As long as questions crowd your mind, there will be doubts in your mind. And as long as you have doubts, your faith will be hindered.

I know from my own experience on a bed of sickness that there were questions in my mind that had to be settled before my faith could be effective. I had to find the answers myself. That is the reason I was bedfast 16 months from ages 15 to 17.

Sometimes it would take me weeks and months to find the answer to a question, and just about the time I found one answer, the devil would bring up something else.

For a long time the devil tried to tell me that God had afflicted me and was punishing me for some wrongdoing in my life. I listened to this for a while, but finally I said, "Devil, I was born this way. I was born with a deformed heart and serious internal trouble. What would be the use of God's punishing me for something I don't even know about? That must not be true."

Sometimes the devil would say, "You're sick because of something your parents did." That is what the disciples thought of the man who was blind from birth. They asked Jesus, *"Master, who did sin, this man, or his parents, that he was born blind?"* (John 9:2)

Some people misquote Jesus' reply in verse 3 as "Neither the man nor his parents sinned. He was sick just so God could heal him." That is not what this Scripture says. It says, *"but that the works of God should be made manifest in him. I must work the works of him that sent me . . . . "* (vv. 3,4).

If a person stopped reading at this point, he might say, "He is sick just so God can heal him." Wouldn't that be a terrible thing to accuse God of? Here is a grown man, blind from birth, and God made him blind just so He could heal him? If that were true, God would not be much of a God, would He? And I would not be interested in

Him. But thank God, that is not true!

Notice that Jesus said, *"I must work the works of him that sent me."* He immediately did the works of God by healing the man.

When the devil saw that I was going to believe in healing anyway, he tried to convince me that it was not God's will to heal me. He said, "Healing is real, but it is *not* God's will to heal *everybody*. *You're* one of those it is *not* His will to heal."

(Many people believe the lie that it is not God's will to heal them, yet it is illogical to believe that God heals, and at the same time believe that He won't heal *you*.)

I rejected this argument, too. I kept searching for answers.

All I knew was what I had heard preachers and other people say. Some said, "Your sickness is God's work. God is doing all of it." I could not accept this explanation. Others said, "Well, maybe God didn't *commission* it, but He *permits* it for a purpose." That is about the same thing.

I never was happy as a child. I never laughed. My daddy left us when I was 6. Being ill affected me emotionally. I was so weak I couldn't defend myself from the other children at school. Everybody could beat me up—even the girls.

When I tried to fight back, the extra effort caused me to faint, because my heart didn't beat right. Many times I was unconscious 45 minutes, and once I was out for an hour and a half. The school nurse and my teacher told me sometimes I would turn black, and sometimes I would be just as blue as I could be. They had to work long and hard to bring me around.

Because of my physical condition and because of my getting pushed around so much, by the time I went into the second grade, I was mad at everybody. I was mad at the whole world. It twisted my thinking.

One day during the noon hour I decided to take things into my own hands. I went off the school grounds to some buildings that had just been built, and I returned with a 2x4 about 20 inches long. I slipped up behind the bully of the playground and hit him right behind the ear as hard as I could. He was out 45 minutes.

I did my best to kill him. At 8 years of age, I thoroughly *meant* to kill him—and I was *disappointed* that I had not.

This was one of several such incidents. I would not fight anybody openly, but as soon as they turned their back, I would knock them in the head with a hammer or whatever else I could get my hands on. I would just as soon have killed them as looked at them. You get tired of getting walked over after a while. Of course, I was not saved then. It makes a lot of difference when the love of God comes into your heart.

I was born again while bedfast, but even after that, questions arose in my mind: *Why was I born this way? Is God the author of the sufferings that are in this world today?* I remember asking myself: *Who is responsible for all of this?*

"Why me?" I asked God.

"Why did I have to be born as a premature baby who weighed less than two pounds? Did You cause me to be born prematurely?

"Why did I have to be afflicted all my life? Why couldn't I have had a normal childhood? Did You rob me of my childhood?

"Why couldn't I have known happiness? Are You the One who caused me to sit and watch as others ran, jumped, and played?"

"Now I am bedfast, and five doctors say I

have to die. Why me? I didn't have anything to do with it. God, did You?"

I wept, "Oh, God, surely I don't have to die! I don't know what it is to live yet. I know what it is to be hungry, cold, and without clothes, but I have never known what it is to be comfortable and to have nice things." (I had been so hungry as a child that the smell of food would make me fall over in a dead faint.)

I said, "I always have been pushed from pillar to post. I never have known what it is to have a family. I had hopes of growing up, marrying, and having a family, but I will never know what it is if I die now. Do I have to die?"

Such questions demand an answer, but nobody really gives you an answer; they will give you some theological concept that does not amount to anything.

But thank God, the Bible has the answer. We can believe God's Word and be delivered, or we can doubt it if we want to and remain bound.

I am so glad I found the answer. I found it in Acts 10:38, *"God anointed Jesus of Nazareth with the Holy Ghost and with power: who went about doing good, and healing all that were oppressed of the devil; for God was with him."*

Jesus went about **doing good, and healing all who were oppressed of the devil.** That is good, isn't it?

This verse told me that Satan is the oppressor . . . Satan is the one who caused me to be born prematurely . . . Satan is the one who caused me to have a deformed heart . . . Satan is the one who caused my body to be almost totally paralyzed . . . Satan is the one who gave me an incurable blood disease . . . Satan is the one who kept me bound for 16 months on a bed of sickness.

But Jesus is the Deliverer!

Jesus is the Lifegiver!

Jesus is the Savior!

Jesus is God manifested in the flesh!

Hallelujah! I never was so thrilled with anything in my life as when I discovered this truth! Yes, God's Word is truth.

After I saw what the Bible said and received my healing, I crawled out of bed and said, "I am not going to die! I am going to live, and someday I am going to have a family—a wife and children."

I was 17 years old then—just a boy. I had never heard healing preached in my life.

My relatives warned me to be careful, but the Bible said it, I believed it, and that settled it. I told everyone I met what I was going to do. People did not want to believe my healing, however. They said I had stayed in bed so long that I had lost my mind.

Today I am the result of what I said in those days. I have enjoyed perfect health ever since. God gave me a lovely wife and family, and it has been heaven all the way. Faith works. That is the reason I get happy preaching about it. I know what He has done for me.

Chapter 2
DON'T BLAME GOD

It is difficult for people who are not acquainted with the Scriptures to understand that the natural laws governing the earth today largely came into being with the fall of man, when Adam sinned and the earth was cursed.

These natural laws, as we understand them, were set aside by Jesus whenever it was necessary to bless humanity. When Satan is finally bound and put in the bottomless pit, all of these laws will cease.

Because people do not understand these laws, many blame God for causing accidents, the sickness and death of loved ones, and such natural catastrophes as storms, earthquakes, and floods. Even insurance companies call natural disasters "acts of God," but they are not acts of God at all!

God is not responsible for any of these

things; neither is He the author of any of them. God is not the author of death. God is not to blame.

Accidents, disease, sickness, death, and disasters come as a result of the fall of man. Their author is Satan.

Adam knew no sickness before he knew sin and Satan.

Dr. John Alexander Dowie, who helped reintroduce divine healing to the Church in this century, said, "Disease (is) the foul offspring of its father, Satan, and its mother Sin."

In the 1870s, when Dr. Dowie was pastoring a Congregational church in a suburb of Sydney, a terrible plague swept through Western Australia. People died like flies.

Years later, Dr. Dowie recalled[1] how he sat in his study one day, his head on his arms, sobbing his heart out before God and asking such questions as: "God, are You the author of sickness and disease? Did You send this terrible plague on this land? Are You going to destroy my whole congregation? Where did this plague come from? Who is the cause of it?"

Dr. Dowie had buried forty of his congregation. Four more awaited burial, and he had just returned home from visiting more than thirty parishioners who were sick and dying.

"Then the words of the Holy Ghost inspired in Acts 10:38 stood before me all radiant with light, revealing Satan as the Defiler, and Christ as the Healer," wrote this man of God.

"My tears were wiped away," Dr. Dowie said, "my heart was strong. I saw the way of healing, and the door thereto was opened wide, so I said, 'God help me now to preach the Word to all the dying around, and tell them how 'tis Satan still defiles, and Jesus still delivers, for "He is just the same today." ' "

He did not have long to wait. Within minutes, two young men burst into his study, pleading breathlessly, "Oh, come at once. Mary is dying!" Dr. Dowie ran down the street after them, not even pausing to take his hat. He was furious that Satan should have attacked this innocent young member of his flock. He found the girl in convulsions.

As Dr. Dowie entered Mary's room, her medical doctor, having given up on her, was preparing to leave. He turned to Dr. Dowie and remarked, "Sir, are not God's ways mysterious?"

The Word of God was burning in Dr. Dowie's heart. "*God's* way!" he thundered. "How *dare* you call that God's way! No, sir, that is *the devil's* work!"

He challenged the physician, who was a member of his congregation, "Can you pray the prayer of faith that saves the sick?"

The doctor replied, "You are much too excited, sir, 'tis best to say God's will be done." And he left.

(Isn't that strange? Many do not believe it is opposing God's will to be kept alive as long as possible by medicine, machines, and every other means, but they believe that *praying* to stay alive is working against God! And when people do die, they call it God's *will!)*

Still furious at Satan's attack, Dr. Dowie prayed the prayer of faith. The girl's convulsions ceased immediately, and she fell into such a deep sleep that her mother and her nurse both thought she had died. "She isn't dead," Dr. Dowie assured them. After several minutes, he awakened Mary. She turned to her mother, and exclaimed, "Mother, I feel so well!"

Remembering how Jesus had ministered to the little girl He had raised from the dead in

Scripture, Dr. Dowie asked, "And you're hungry?"

"Oh, yes," she agreed. "I'm so hungry."

He instructed the nurse to fix Mary a cup of hot chocolate and some bread and butter. Then he went into the next room, where her brother and sister lay sick with the same fever.

After prayer, they, too, instantly recovered. From that day on, Dr. Dowie ministered to his flock on divine healing and prayed for their healing. He never lost another member to the plague.

"As I went away from the home where Christ as the Healer had been victorious," Dr. Dowie wrote, "I could not but have somewhat in my heart of the triumphant song that rang through Heaven, and yet I was not a little amazed at my own strange doings, and still more at my discovery that HE IS JUST THE SAME TODAY. And this is the story of how I came to preach the Gospel of Healing through Faith in Jesus."

---

[1]Gordon Lindsay, *The Life of John Alexander Dowie* (The Voice of Healing Publishing Co., 1951), pp. 22-26. (Now known as Christ for the Nations, Box 24910, Dallas, Tex. 75224.)

Chapter 3
REDEEMED FROM THE CURSE

The Bible pictures Jesus as the *Deliverer* of men and women—**not as their destroyer.** That is the revelation Dr. Dowie saw that day: *Satan* is the destroyer. *Jesus* is the Deliverer.

In his first Epistle, John says, concerning Jesus, *"For this purpose the Son of God was manifested, that he might destroy the works of the devil"* (1 John 3:8).

Again, the Bible says in Luke 9:56, *"For the Son of man is not come to* ***destroy*** *men's lives, but to* ***save*** *them."*

A year or two ago, I received a lovely letter from a young woman who was about to be paroled from prison.

She wrote that when she was 5, her parents broke up, and she went to live with her father. He lived with a succession of different women, and by the time this girl was 13, she was out on the streets—a prostitute. Then she got into dope.

At 17 she married a man much older than herself for protection and security. At 18 she had a child. At 19 she was arrested and sent to the penitentiary for peddling dope.

"During all these years I was very bitter," she said. "I blamed God for my parents breaking up. I blamed God for the kind of life I had and for all the bad things that had happened.

"When I got to prison, my cellmate had your magazine, *The Word of Faith*. She tried to witness to me, but I wouldn't listen to her, and I wouldn't read the magazine.

"One day when she wasn't in the cell, I read the magazine, and the first message was 'Don't Blame God.' I saw that it was the devil who had robbed me of a mother, who had caused my home to be divided, and who had caused all my misery, suffering, and heartache. I got mad at the devil for lying to me.

"I got down on my knees, gave my heart to God, and was born again.

"My cellmate and I wrote in for your literature. We were both baptized in the Holy

Spirit. We began a prayer meeting, and we got 39 other prisoners saved and filled with the Spirit. Even the Roman Catholic chaplain became filled with the Spirit. I want to thank you for bringing truth to me."

She went on to say that she would return to her husband and child after her release from prison. Her husband also had been saved and baptized in the Holy Spirit, and the couple planned to go into the ministry.

Reading her letter, I thought about this principle of not blaming God, but I also thought about the Scripture *"ye shall know the truth, and the truth shall make you free"* (John 8:32). The truth had set her free.

Jesus said in John 10:10, *"I am come that they might have life, and that they might have it more abundantly."* He added, *"The thief* (Satan) *cometh not, but for to steal, and to kill, and to destroy."*

In this verse, Jesus is contrasting the works of God with the works of the devil. You see, that which *steals*—that which *kills*—that which **destroys**—is the devil's work. That is plain enough, isn't it?

Jesus made another profound statement in

this verse when He said, *"I am come . . . ."*

Who is He?

The Bible teaches that **Jesus is God manifested in the flesh.** In John 14:9, Jesus said, *"Have I been so long time with you, and yet hast thou not known me, Philip?* ***he that hath seen me hath seen the Father.****"*

Today we trust radio, television, magazines, and newspapers to tell us what leading personalities are "really like." If you want to know what God is "really like," look at Jesus. God is just like Jesus. Jesus said, *"he that hath seen me hath seen the Father."*

Furthermore, **if you want to see God at work, look at Jesus.** In John 14:10, Jesus said, *"Believest thou not that I am in the Father, and the Father in me? the words that I speak unto you I speak not of myself: but* ***the Father that dwelleth in me, he doeth the works****."*

The way the Father, working in Jesus, healed people was *through the anointing of the Holy Spirit.* We read in Acts 10:38 that God anointed Jesus with the Holy Spirit and power—healing power—and He went about doing good and healing all who were oppressed of the devil. These are the works of God. (This and other Scriptures plainly call sickness Satanic oppression.)

When Jesus said, "*the Father . . . doeth the works,*" it meant that He did *all* of the works that Jesus did. For example, when Jesus was aboard that tiny boat in the Sea of Galilee and rebuked the storm (Mark 4:39), it actually was the Father rebuking the storm through Jesus.

Well, if God *caused* the storm, God would be working against Himself if He *rebuked* it! The same holds true with healings. If God is the author of sickness and disease, yet God healed people through Jesus, then God would be working against Himself! (And Jesus said in Mark 3:24,25 that a house divided against itself cannot stand.)

Jesus' description of the Father in the 14th chapter of John; His statement in the 9th verse of that chapter *("he that hath seen me hath seen the Father");* His statement in the 10th verse *("the Father that dwelleth in me, he doeth the works");* and the Scripture from Acts 10 *("he went about doing good, and healing all that were oppressed by the devil")* make it impossible for me to accept the teaching that disease and sickness are of God. The very nature of God the

Father refutes that argument.

Jesus plainly taught in these and other Scriptures that disease and sickness are of Satan.

Let us examine the 13th chapter of Luke's Gospel, for example. Here, Jesus was in a synagogue when a woman who was *"bowed together"* entered. The Bible says *"she could in no wise lift up herself."* I suppose she had arthritis or some disease of that nature, because her body was locked in a bent position.

Jesus called the woman to Himself and said, *"Woman, thou art loosed from thine infirmity."* Then He touched her. Evidently God's healing power was transmitted by that touch into her body. She straightened up and was instantly healed.

The synagogue leader became angry, pretending that his anger was because Jesus had healed on the Sabbath. Jesus made a profound statement in reply. He said, *"Ought not this woman, being a daughter of Abraham, whom Satan hath bound, lo, these eighteen years, be loosed from this bond on the sabbath day?"*(v. 16).

Jesus said three positive statements here:

(1) *Satan* had bound this woman the entire eighteen years; (2) Jesus said she ought to be loosed; and (3) the reason she ought to be loosed was because she was a daughter of Abraham.

"Yes," somebody might say, "healing belonged to the Jews." (Anytime you get a good Scripture that promises you physical, material, and financial prosperity or blessing, somebody always says, "That was just for the Jews.") Well, wait a minute.

Turn to Galatians 3:13,14: *"Christ hath redeemed us from the curse of the law, being made a curse for us: for it is written, Cursed is every one that hangeth on a tree:* ***That the blessing of Abraham might come on the Gentiles*** *through Jesus Christ."* Now look at the 29th verse: *"And* ***if ye be Christ's, then are ye Abraham's seed,*** *and heirs according to the promise."*

Are you Christ's? Are you His? You know that does not mean you are Abraham's *physical* seed or physical descendant. But if you are Christ's—if you have been born again—you are Abraham's *spiritual* seed, and you have fallen heir to the promise.

Now look at the 7th verse of this chapter:

"Know ye therefore that ***they which are of faith,*** *the same* ***are the children of Abraham."***

Jesus said, "This woman ought to be loosed from her infirmity because she is a child of Abraham." And God is saying the same thing today: "You (spiritual) sons and daughters of Abraham ought not to be bound by sickness or disease. You ought to be free."

Thank God, Jesus came to redeem us from the hand of Satan, from sin, and from sickness, because ***Jesus came to redeem us from the curse of the law*** (Gal. 3:13).

To find out what the curse of the law is, we must go back to the law—the first five books of the Bible. There we will find that the curse of the law is *poverty, sickness,* and *death.*

God established a covenant with the children of Israel as they were en route to the Promised Land after coming out of Egypt.

God warned them that if they refused to walk in His statutes and keep His commandments they would suffer many afflictions (Deuteronomy 28:15-68).

If they were obedient, however, God promised, *"And ye shall serve the Lord your God, and he shall bless thy bread, and thy water; and*

I will take sickness away from the midst of thee. *There shall nothing cast their young, nor be barren, in thy land:* ***the number of thy days I will fulfil"*** (Exod. 23:25,26).

People believe you must get sick to die, but God did not say so.

God said He would fulfill the number of their days. He did not say they were *not* going to die—but He said they would not have to die because of sickness or disease.

Healing belongs to us under the New Covenant (or New Testament) just as it belonged to Israel under the Old. New Testament believers *are* redeemed now from spiritual death. We *are* redeemed from sickness and from poverty. And we have the promise that when Jesus comes again, physical death will be put under foot. To make it more personal:

Healing belongs to you.

It belongs to you because sickness is of the enemy.

It belongs to you because you are a spiritual child of Abraham.

It belongs to you because sickness is a curse, and Christ has redeemed you from the curse of the law.

Chapter 4
"DON'T DIE LIKE THIS!"

After my wife and I arrived at a new pastorate in northcentral Texas, the church pianist asked me to visit a woman everybody called "Grandma." Grandma was in a nearby hospital dying of stomach cancer. She was 82.

We were busy moving into the parsonage. Several days went by. That Wednesday, I had an impression to call Grandma's family, because I somehow knew they had taken her home. I didn't know why they would, because the family already had told me that they were going to keep her in the hospital until she died. I called, and her daughter confirmed that Grandma had talked the doctor into sending her home to die.

I went to visit Grandma. She was a woman who knew about divine healing. She had been healed years before, and the healing had brought her into the baptism of the Holy Spirit.

I began to talk to her about letting God heal her.

"Oh, Brother Hagin," she said, "I'm saved and filled with the Spirit, and I'm ready for heaven. Just let me alone and let me die."

I said, "I'm not going to do it. Grandma, it is not the will of God that you die this way; no one will ever make me believe that. It is not the will of God that you die with cancer and suffer this way. Let God heal you and *then* die if you want to—but don't die like this!"

Friends, you are not going to get somebody healed if you are believing they will live, and they are believing they will die. As the Bible says, *"Can two walk together, except they be agreed?"* (Amos 3:3)

I knew Grandma was not ready to receive healing, so I read Scripture to her, knelt by her bed, laid my hand on her head, and prayed, "Dear God, help Grandma not to cast away her confidence. She knows about divine healing. It was a healing that brought her into the baptism of the Holy Spirit years ago."

I returned two or three times every week,

prayed that way, read God's Word to her, and tried to talk her out of dying. And she kept living.

We had healing services every Saturday night, and about every three weeks Grandma would say to her son-in-law, "Get me up, make a bed in the car, and take me to church."

We would take a large chair out of the parsonage and place pillows around her. Grandma sat on the side near the piano, and many times in these services, right in the middle of my sermon, she would have a spell, and you would think she was dead.

This went on about every three weeks. I visited her several times a week. Six months went by. One Saturday night during my sermon I looked over at Grandma—and I *perceived* something. You know, Paul was preaching at Lystra, and Paul *perceived* (Acts 14:9) that a man crippled from birth had faith to be healed.

I *perceived* that Grandma's faith had risen to the level where she had faith to be healed. So I stopped my sermon, looked her way, and said, "Grandma, it wouldn't surprise me at all to see you out of that chair healed, dancing like a 16 year old." When I said that to her, the Lord gave me a vision. In the vision, as I stood right there at the pulpit, I saw her jump out of the chair and dance like a girl.

I said, "We'll pray for you right now and start the healing service." I went down, anointed her with oil, laid hands on her, and prayed for her. There was no manifestation of her healing at first, so we started the healing line. After we had been praying for the sick about 10 minutes, suddenly I heard somebody say, "Praise the Lord!" I looked around, and Grandma had jumped out of that chair.

She ran halfway across the building, started dancing a jig for joy like a 16-year-old girl, and was healed. In 30 days' time, praise God, she had put on so much weight that you couldn't recognize her.

Several years later, we were on the evangelistic field, and because our children were joining us for the summer, we took Ken's collie dog to friends in the country. We had to go right by Grandma's house, and my wife suggested, "Why don't we stop and see Grandma?" This was 9 years later, and Grandma was 91.

We visited with Grandma's daughter, supposing that Grandma was in her room. Finally my wife asked to see Grandma.

"Oh," her daughter said, "you know Ma. She's just like she always was. She's off gallivanting around the country. She's visiting some of the kinfolks in another part of the country, and she rode the bus to get there. She is never at home."

I learned later that Grandma lived until she was 93, and she went home to be with Jesus *without* sickness or disease. She had lived 11 more years.

Most people would have said, "We might as well go ahead and die. After all, God only promised us 70 or 80 years." Yes, He did. And, yes, you are going to die sometime—but ***you do not have to die with sickness and disease.*** Not if you are one of Abraham's spiritual descendants.

I know God's Word. God's Word works.

In the Old Testament, God set life and death before the children of Israel. He said, *"I call heaven and earth to record this day against you, that I have set before you life and death, blessing and cursing: therefore* ***choose life,*** *that both thou and thy seed may live"* (Deut. 30:19).

Chapter 5
SECRET THINGS

People have asked me why some of my relatives did not get healed. I have asked the Lord the same question.

"That is a secret between them and Me," the Lord told me once when I prayed about it. He said very plainly, "It's none of your business. You keep preaching healing and leave that question alone. Don't even touch it in your thought life."

Sometimes there is a reason why a person does not get healed. It is a private matter between them and the Lord, and He does not tell everyone else about it. The Bible says in Deuteronomy 29:29, "*The secret things belong unto the Lord our God: but those things which are revealed belong unto us. . . .*"

After my sister died at age 55 of cancer, I lay on my bed, meditating. Suddenly it seemed like I left my body. I was up in heaven.

My sister and Jesus were standing talking. Her back was to me. I don't know what Jesus was saying, but when He saw me, He stopped talking and looked at me. My sister turned and looked, too.

She said, "Kenneth, don't feel so badly that you couldn't pray the prayer of faith for me. There was a reason you couldn't. I suffered a lot, but since it's all over and I'm here, I wouldn't have it any other way. You couldn't help me, but you *can* help Joy" (her daughter).

In the Spirit, I saw myself ministering that coming Sunday night to my niece. (This vision took place on Thursday night.)

We buried my sister on Saturday. On Sunday night, the pastor said, "I don't know what it is, Brother Hagin, but God wants you to do something. Feel free to do whatever it is."

I told the congregation what I had seen in my vision. I called Joy forward. (Joy had had numerous shock treatments. She walked around like a robot. We had to give her such elementary instructions as "Put your arm down" and "Close your mouth.") I found myself casting three devils out of Joy. Her whole countenance changed. She has been completely free ever since.

I still don't know why I could not help my sister. But we know according to Scripture that God was not to blame for her death.

I knew a pastor who was very strong on preaching that healing belongs to all of us. A woman asked him, "How can you be so positive it is the will of God to heal everybody when you lost your only daughter when she was 13?"

The pastor replied, "Well, first of all, I believe that if we had known then what we know now, she would not have died. Second, we haven't lost her. She's over in Father's house. Third, we didn't lose the battle; we just lost that one round. I stand in faith."

A lot of times we wait until it is too late to do something. Hope says, "I'll get healed *sometime.*" Heart faith says, "It's mine *now.*"

About seven years after a certain pastor's wife died of cancer at an early age, I held a meeting in that church. A death pall still hung over the church. The people were all bewildered about her death.

After I ministered that week, the pastor said, "You've just lifted a cloud off my shoulders about my wife's dying with cancer. She was in the ministry with me. She was a holy woman; a great woman of prayer. I blamed God for her death.

"But she never did believe she *was* healed. She always believed she was *going to get* healed. She kept pushing it off into the future, and the disease took its course. She died saying, 'I believe God *is going to* heal me.'

"At the time, I thought that was faith," the pastor said, "but I see now that was not Bible faith."

Christians do not take advantage of what belongs to them. Either they do not know *how* to take advantage of what belongs to them, or they do not know *what* belongs to them.

Deliverance belongs to us *now*—not in some far-off day somewhere, sometime.

We will not need healing in heaven or in the Millennium. We can have it now . . . in this world . . . in this age . . . in this life . . . because Jesus already *has* purchased healing for our body as well as salvation for our soul.

God laid on Jesus not only the sin, sickness, and disease of us all, but also the cause of that sickness and disease. And what He bore, we do not need to bear.